Death of a Black Star

Sharday Cage

Also Released by Sakura Publishing

When Heaven Calls

Fortino

Touretties

Lost Evidents

Dump Your Problems!

The Legend of Willow Springs Farm

Stricken Yet Crowned

"Did I Really Do My Hair for This?"

Death of a Black Star

Sharday Cage

Sakura Publishing

 Published in the United States by Sakura Publishing, Pennsylvania, in 2011. http://www.sakura-publishing.com

Table of Contents

Foreword
Milo Samardzija

My advertising business fell victim to the economic meltdown that occurred late in the first decade of this century, so I had to take a temporary night job until things picked up.

It wasn't a great job. I had never done anything like it before. I won't even mention what it was except to say it was not a position I'd care to post on my resume. The best thing about it was the hours, six hours a night, four days a week. It allowed me to keep my normal activities going during the day, while providing much-needed extra cash. It was exactly what I needed at the time.

The business wasn't truly fly-by-night, but it was close. The work force was a mixed bag of interesting characters. There were middle managers who had been downsized, kids working their way through college, retirees supplementing their incomes, a few whores who were too old to make a decent living, musicians who had wasted their youths trying to get record deals, actors who were between roles, several young men with crude, jailhouse tattoos, some folks who were impossible to explain or describe, and, of course, one aging, burned-out advertising man.

It seemed that anyone that wanted the job could have it. The only requirements were literacy and minimal computer skills. Turnover was ferocious. None of the employees stayed very long.

One day I was eating lunch in the noisy, crowded break room and chatting with a couple of friends, one who had been a bank robber and the other who was struggling with his crack addiction, when I heard a voice that stopped me in mid-sentence. It was the voice of an angel, sweet, clear, and ringing with portent. It took a few moments for me to realize that what I was hearing was a young woman reading poetry of astonishing power and beauty to a small group of enthralled listeners.

I listened to the young woman read a few more poems and decided that I had to meet her. When I introduced myself she told me that her name was Sharday Cage and that the poems were, indeed, of her own composition.

When I met Sharday, I was, and still am, a partner in a blog site called The Third City, which takes pride in offering writers a platform to present new work. I immediately asked Sharday if she would consider contributing some of her poetry to The Third City. To my great pleasure, she said, "yes."

Over a period of several months, The Third City posted close to a dozen of Sharday's poems – and every one was a gem. Her poems are wise, edgy, funky, relevant, and universal. Best of all, to steal a phrase from the old jazzmen, her poems "swing." She has impeccable pace, rhythm, and timing. Sharday's poetry is a joy to read.

I was not surprised when Sharday received an offer to have her poetry published. I knew it was just a matter of time. What truly surprised me was that Sharday asked me to write a forward to her first published book of poems.

Without hesitation, without a moment's thought, I said yes. Nothing would give me greater pleasure.

I take no credit for discovering Sharday Cage. I simply recognized that her talent was full-blown and undeniable from the moment I heard her reading her poems in the lunch room of that temporary workplace we shared.

What I will accept credit for is spotting greatness early on. Now you can discover Sharday Cage for yourself.

Milo Samardzija, Summer, 2011

Foreword

Abraham Eddie "Master" Mkhatshwa

Africa my beginning; Africa my ending in the spirits of ubuntu (Humanity): Let me praise the illustrious daughter of the soil I first met in Durban (South Africa) on the 15th of August 2007. Vividly I can still see the image of a young, beautiful African lady painting the room with an American accent, yet her soul was pure African in one of the vibrant Wednesday students' poetry sessions. From the personality of Sharday, I was able to learn more about the beauty of life and the cultural diversity shared among the citizens of the world. Yes, her birth was definitely a blessing, not only to her family, but to the whole world.

Sharday Cage: Be forever mindful that in Africa we are living in Dark Ages where shadows of ignorance and imperfect information are in circulation, polluting our worldview, hence the continental ignorance. Night is cold and long, but since your intellectual poetry light is on, the whole world can see clearly the meaning of humanity and morality in principle and actual terms. Lady, through poetry you can speak for those enslaved, tortured, vulnerable souls who cannot speak for themselves. Additionally, your poetic words can be a beacon of hope in a desert of despair. Like a camel's eye, let your poetic courage see life trough desert storms by painting the colour of the global socio-economic injustices and imbalances.

Ubunkondlo isikhali sokulwa impi yobumnyama. ("Poetry is an institution of true defiance, using clinical wisdom to unify the diverse human race.")

The first time I met Sharday, I was still a teenager from Pienaar, Msogwaba, a dysfunctional, poverty-stricken South African township. But through the power of poetry as a mode of self-expression, we were able to build bridges through productive cultural exchange. I still remember vividly that Sharday Cage, Mdu Mtsweni, and Scelo "Bash" Gcabashe were the most highly-gifted poets with their precise, thought-provoking social commentary about issues of global relevance.

Sharday as an individual was an epitome of humanity, a global citizen in every shape and form. She is definitely an agent of change living in a junk, money-driven society, whereby all the social units and citizens of the world have certainly hit a low-point of humanity. But, God had a plan for any human being living under the sun as part and parcel of his quality production line, coupled with divine spiritual architecture. Hence, Sharday's journey to Africa was planned by God Himself. Basically, the Creator was molding, shaping her for life; this lady was destined for greatness, therefore she is an ambassador for humanity and justice across the globe.

She was a fresh, down-to-earth girl from Chicago, only speaking English whereas the majority of us could speak at least seven indigenous languages (from Swati to isiZulu and all the Nguni languages). But, it was a powerful cultural exchange at the end.

Abraham Eddie "Master" Mkhatshwa

Acknowledgements

First and foremost, I must thank the ruler of my life, God. I was given a gift that I can't explain and all I feel is an overwhelming amount of gratitude, joy, and happiness that it was given to me. I truly am thankful for what seems very simple and inexpensive, but to me its worth is invaluable. I've never cared for anything more so I will forever be grateful for the possession of my purpose. To touch someone, move them emotionally, or inspire them, somehow it still brings about a joy I can't get anywhere else. It is a blessing and I wouldn't trade it for anything in the world. God has touched me and filled me with such contentment and complete satisfaction with just words that I can never be ruled by pleasure, which would eventually betray me, and, because of that, I believe He has given me one of the most precious gifts of all.

To my beautiful mother, Laverta Cage, who has been nothing but the epitome of a superwoman. I don't know how you did the things you did but you amaze me, and everything I do will inevitably be because of you. There is no other human on this earth that I love more than you.

To my pops William Visor, I can think of no kinder, sweeter, gentler, more well-mannered man than you. You inspire me every day when it comes to how to talk to someone, how to treat someone with the same respect as you would want back. You're a bigger man than most, and I love you dearly, and I'm proud to have you as my father.

Thank you, Anita, for all your support and a joy that can only belong to a beautiful soul, I am so glad you are part of the family.

Aunt Trish, you are one of the smartest, funniest people in the world, and I love you.

To my brothers, William Cage and Jeremy Visor, I will never let you guys down and you will always be able to count on me. To my cousins, Alicia Sanders and Deanna Cage: All my life you were never really my cousins but you were always, always my sisters. I love you guys.

Thank you, Uncle Johnny, for your constant support and for always saying "no worries". You say it in the greatest of times and in the toughest, and I can't tell you how comforting it is to hear you say that. You are the rock of the family and I know whatever happens, you'll get us through it. Thank you, Shari, for always welcoming me into your beautiful home with absolute love and kindness.

To the rest of my family whom I love: Muffy, Little Ricky, Rick, and the entire Sanders Family; Aneesah, Jayden, Mary-Jo, Mag. and the entire Young Family; Duck, Dimples, Gary, Little Gary, June, Larry, Uncle Bill, Anita, Angela, and the entire Mitchell Family; Kim, Mikey, Brian, Carol, Sherry, Tommy, Eboni, Malcolm, Sarah, Michael, Stevie, Junior, Mary, Annie, Eulus, Connie, and to the rest of my family members who I failed to mention. I love you all.

To Wendy Richards, I can't imagine life on this earth without women like you. It would be the most miserable place. You are so wise, kind, funny, and just completely lovely. You are not only an amazing woman but an amazing person. You have given me so much and have helped me every step of the way. I can only hope to become as great as you. I love you.

To Gabriela Richards, you are my best friend. You will always be my best friend and nothing will ever be more certain to me than this. We will grow old together with cats and dogs, and, if men are still too stupid to realize how incredible we are, at least we'll have each other. You are the one friend that I know I will have to the very end and I am very, very lucky. You are a wonder of the world and no one— I mean no one— can make an entrance like you can. Love you, Gabster!

Special thanks to the rest of the Wognum family, Tom and Nikki, John, Peter, Jim.

To my friends who have inspired me and loved me in spite of it all: thank you for believing in me and never giving up on me. I have gained many and lost the same, but it doesn't change their incredible impact on my life, so I thank those in my life and also those who are not. You all are still in my heart.

In no particular order: Annie and the rest of the Correa family, Nicole Clark, Mallory Clark, Loren Williams, Anna Boyd, Danny Marshall, Joel Robinson, Jena Cooper and the entire Cooper family, April, Fa'Darryl Brown, Thea Logan, Alicia Ivy, Carlton Graham, Arthur Barnes, Tony Brown, Axel, Sabe, Arlena, Aixa, Daisey, Rubio, Jeffery, Gael, Abel, Abby, Juan #1, Juan #2, Douglas, Sbu, Benny J, Milo Samardzija, Samuke, Mrs. Washington, Corey, Tiana and the entire Camphor family, Christian, Vanessa, Grace, Darren, Mrs. D, Ernest, Eunice, Shanna, Gugu, Master, John Bowen, Latrice Karabo, Latrice, Qisoundra, Karyn, Kennia Clarke, Tee, Markia, Kemi, Leeza, Letsatsi, Loretta, Luciana, Mabo, Mrs. Petterson, Maureen, the Fraser family, Jared, Ray Stallworth, Lindelani, Ezael, Sdu, Xolani, Precious, Phil, Mike O, Bryan I, Roberta, Amanda, Ms. Calhoun, Steve W, Valene, Mrs. Richards, Mr.

Parson, Mr. Smith, Ron Mark, and to the rest of my friends whom I failed to mention— thank you for the love and support!

To my brother Bash Gxabhashe, I love you and I hope you enjoy my poems. Now you can see me whenever you wish.

To Amajuoritse Amudoaghan, you always saw something in me that I didn't quite see in myself. You always believed in me. Thank You.

To Eugene Mhoon, for your support, for reading my poems, for your compliments. You really are special to me.

Jared, you for the fire.

RIP Christian Hales and Joanna Jones; they were beginning their dreams but left us too early. It is up to us to finish it for them. With Love.

Special thanks to Derek Vasconi. I couldn't have asked for a better publisher. You came out of nowhere and opened the most beautiful door for me, and you did it like a true gentleman. Without hesitancy, you took a chance on me, and I am so grateful that you did because you helped me achieve my dream. I'll always have this book and I have you partly to thank for that. It's so strange how quickly I trusted you even though I barely knew you, but faith is not yet overrated because it did not fail me. You are a good person, never lose that. You are rare and you are special.

Sarah, you're awesome. The end.

To Matthew Wade, I'm writing this before I've actually seen your illustrations to my book but that sneaky faith tugs at me again, and I just know that whatever you do, I'll fall madly in love with it. I knew the minute I saw your work that you were the one. You are extremely talented and I wish you all the best.

If I forgot anybody, I'm terribly sorry. Just know that in my heart, I have you all tattooed on my chest. I love you all so much. I hope you enjoy the book and pass it on. I am the contents of this book so when you read this, you are reading me.

Dedication

To my beautiful grandmother,

So in heaven they will know I did not forget about you.

Introduction

I am a black star. One who is often inspired by everything that has somehow ignited my path. I examine everything in wonderment, dissecting it with my eyes, whereby I give it my unique perspective. All that has moved me, changed me, molded on to me can be read in this compilation of poetry, wherein I give you my complete honesty and purest truth. I cannot lie in my poetry nor would I want to, because I want my truth to pour out of the page so you can feel exactly how I feel. Essentially, I want to raise emotions and thoughts out of you that you didn't know you had.

I am a black star. At times when I was young or growing up in a small town, I felt indifferent or invisible. Always one or the other; I was there amongst a crowd, present as an oddity or not there at all. I would wonder who would look at me with wonderment and say she was black and beautiful or black and bright. Was I worth your wish? Do you believe in me? I moved to Chicago and found a light within myself that no darkness could dim, but I was overwhelmed by the cities of Chicago, especially the youth within them and their need to be lit. There are millions of black stars hiding within the dark, unaware of their potential to shine, to be more than what they are. The crippling night is what they feed off of, possibly because it's all they believe they have.

Have we betrayed them somehow...all these black stars that are falling? Is it beyond our power that the night, ruler of everything, has made a plot to kill them off and we too weak to save them? When the darkness comes, we should not fear it but fight it and secure a light inside ourselves and light everyone else along with it...so then the dark will never own us. A spark of hope, faith, truth, and life will mark a path to show us the way. We have to light our black stars before it's too late.

This book is dedicated to all the black stars, and this book is in part a start to that light.

Death of the Black Star

During dark reasoning
The night, our conspirator,
Rose against the black star,
Her own children.

Purposefully unashamed
The ruler of the first black,
Our night,
Without remorse
Aborted her black stars,
Keeping only the cloud and moon at peace
As the decorators of heaven.

Loosed from home,
Like a detached stranger,
Released from the love once demanded,
The black star turns to weeping,
Spiraling like a dying bird
Towards the unaware.

Don't wish upon the fallen black star,
For your wishes will bring death,
Never to come true.
The broken winged fliers
Disconnected with the earth—
Gravity holds them no more.

One by one
Black stars fall by the millions,
Crashing among us.
We that let them fall.
With a thud, they cover the earth.

The black rain will ruin us all.
It has already begun,
The debris of the black star.

The tragedy is not that of
living so high
And falling so far,
But to have lived so high
Yet never glow.
Rotted early of their radiance,
The black stars were exiled from the
sky.

Already the night claimed the dark
expanding,
And found nothing extraordinary
about them.
Plummeting to an untimely death,
Unwanted, abandoned—
Death of the black star.

It has already begun,
Beneath our feet,
Black stars slumber,
Their sleep disturbing,
Like fish ashore.

Their death has become a path we
walk on.
A path we walk over.
Their fate, a mere residue,
Found on the soles of our shoes.

I Am Afraid

I am afraid for the black man
With his unattended braids
Lost in the roughness of his hair
And the scent of weed
Fragranced on his skin
Sending an internal fear in the mind of whites
And the havoc it wills
To be alarmed of his black
Build hate amongst him
So in turn he should hate himself
I am afraid of his pitch black eyes with nothing to see
But the vastness of emptiness
Lost in the inertia of going nowhere
While remaining still
As time ticks on
Stuck in a moment that belongs to death
Killing a man that never began
I am afraid of his wanting
The chasing of societal dreams
And still not dreamt his own
And so the residue of a fake glory remains
Except the black man believes in this fame
Soaking up its pretending light
That a woman is nothing but her face and her shape
Her large breast and her voluptuous curves
To worship the light-skinned woman

(Who resembles the white-skinned woman)
That a rapper should be his savior
(That it is all the black man should strive to be)
Without integrity but zealous for the diamond and Lamborghini
Without decency in his own country
But to money his fulfilling need
I am afraid for the black man
Who is easily influenced
I am afraid for the black man because he accepted the world's lies
Only to surrender to such a cumbersome demise
The perfect scheme became the dream he dreamed
I am afraid of the black man who is scared to be
I am afraid for the black man for I fear he is not yet free

black bird

black bird

fly for the child

with the missing

wings

go tell God of the

broken boy

or the cracked girl

dancing to a silent

song

and when the music

plays

it is but the rhythm

of soft crying

mourning a whisper

to stop the dance

that will not end

black bird

fly for the child

stuck in a dance

a beautiful waltz

we watch them die

too.

Fourth of July

Look at us
Crowded and doomed
Wide-eyed
Like an electrocuted fly
Peering up
At the vacant sky
Searching for a firework
That will bring us to life
The **boom**
That will jumpstart
Our **heart** again
And revive our lost eyes
To a **light** unrealized
A burst of color
To shroud the darkened **wonder**
Into red flames
Or yellow **rays**
To be more than this imminent grey
That is merely a peaceful **portrait**
Of you and I
Watch and **spy**
And you will see
We are nothing but a **violent image**
Of the midnight sky
Look at us
A crowded divide
All **gazing** at
The intergalactic wide
Awaiting the boom

Like a suitable answer
To our **questions** gloom
Words that hide in our mouth
Resting **there**
In the form of a depressed peace
Silenced and **hidden**
The pains of our burdens
Though many of us can **see**
Through our shiny sheer curtains
And it is painfully **obvious**
That we are troubled here
Amongst **one** another
That we are uncomfortable
Here **with** each other
But for one night
We put **our** troubles aside
To unite
For the **Fourth of July**

To Mister John Doe

I can only imagine
Your twisted smile
Slowly destructing
Into its ill-fitted frown
That suits you so well
When you see
What I've done
I came to wreak
A heavenly havoc
On the disaster you made
And transform your death
Into life's breath
A rebirth
And a new generation
That will not stop
Until your destruction dances
Into a beautiful show
Until your corruption dissolves
And the earth made aglow
I will not die
Until I have formed cities of your opposite
Ghettos will turn to gold
And children will die old
And you will see
Everything that you are will not grow

And there will be not one seed with an evil soul.

Come Rise with Me

Come rise with me

And set a flame

The death that comes for you

Take note of its fear

And write that you live on

And your breath

Still sweet with courage

Hide not alongside

Those who wait to die

Fill your heart

With the will

To be

More than nothing

More than something

Your nightmare is powerless

But for the scenery it dreams up

Find your eyes

And kill its vision

Be a conqueror in your sleep

So your walk

May be victorious in the morning

Find pride in your light

And never dim

Into the luxury of night's sin

society.

Don't spend forever
Searching for distractions
Following the life of someone
Discovering the death of no one

Practice the law of light
And chase your dreams
Depend on society
And you will fail
Never a friend
But a quiet enemy
A soft whisper
To strike the mind ill
A poison too subtle
For one to notice a kill
Society is but
A cold kiss
On warm lips
You will freeze to death
Upon its touch

Find your life
And make it invaluable
Worth more than gold
And not one man can touch you

But put a price on your soul
And death is near

The Happening

Until the thing I love to do becomes
the vocal point of my life
I am a slave
The russet chains overtake my body
But where I sit bound
The keys lay not too far from me
They shimmer with freedom
I understand I must suffer for a time
But when that time comes when I'm
set free
With appreciative laugh and a
humble cry
And a celebrative dance
I will shout about from the mountain
tops

Behold, my liberty

The Light

Surrender to the light
And allow it to consume you whole
Take in the brightness of a new day
With breath comes life
Inhale
Smell the scent of the sun
In it forgiveness and love
No longer shackled by the past
Today you are free
And you are beautiful

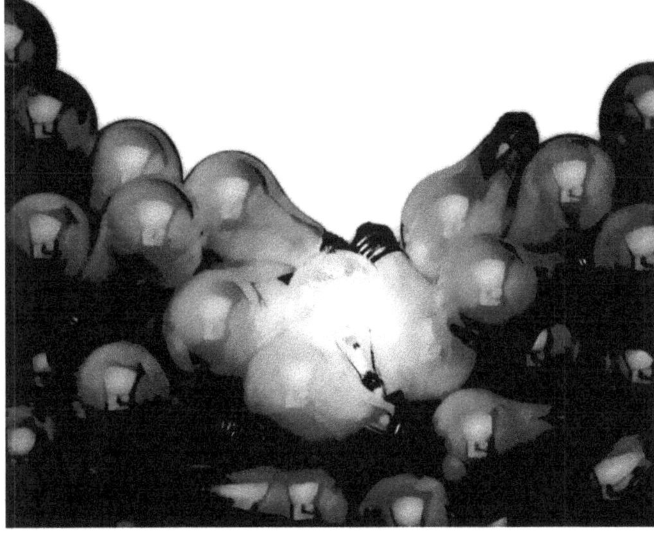

Portrait

I have seen images
Painted with the same color
That paints me
And the vision
I loathed
Because it was the ugliest picture
I have ever seen
Yet equally I loved
Because it was the most beautiful picture
I have ever seen
This picture of me so imperfectly
A face distorted
Yet rewarded as a masterpiece
Disproportioned
A people shunned
With a weary walk
And a sad talk
Every drawing
Disconnected and helpless
Each detail disguised in depression
Dependent on your outline
Desperate for your colors
In need of your background
Though you were anxious
To create an ugly me
To forever hide in your mockery
That lived your intentional lie
Those paintings were drawn to destroy me
And those who look like me
We were supposed to self- destruct in them
But to some the ugly was beautiful
And art we became
We outlived your vengeance
Suspected your suspense
We survived your two cents
And regained our innocence

Meaningful Meaningless

From afar
Echoes hark
And a valley stood dull
Whistling, a singing skull
Painted in a broken mirror
Poised in a depressed view
A somber solitude
As rotten mountains frown
And decadent bones lay 'round
Were a handful of meaningful words
Cursed
Buried within the earth immersed
Their meanings hollow
As deaf ears swallow
Professing instead
Words of emptiness
And shallowness
Running rampant through the open air
Their whispers, a musical chair
A dance to mock you
To sympathize with its rule
To unleash its sins
Amongst the living world
The surviving pearl
While hope and faith
An echo too distant to stay
So meaningless words have risen

And their reign has begun
A meaningless prison
To celebrate
Their words torched the sky
Blotting out the sun
Hate became the new love
And death the new life
Meaningless became the new
meaningful
Now we are slaves to negativity
Feeding off their insincerity
All becoming fake and ill
We'll relish in sorrow
And walk in a weariness tomorrow
Who will be so bold to deny this fate?
Who will put an end to our funeral, our
wake?
And seek humility
Humanity
Who will rise up?
And journey to
A life more than this
Meaningful meaningless
Who will walk through the valley
Of the shadow of death
And find the truth that was left
To seek out the words of life
To obtain them
And set them free

When the Dark Comes

During that late hour
Of horrid winds
And thunderous storms
The shadows came
Offering only bitterness and regret
Though your heart had been broken
Many times before
And your wounds cut deeply
You found no reason to join them
You walked beneath a starless sky
And into the valley
But your heart remained lit
And set a path
God knew a day like this would come
So before you existed
Inside your mother's womb
He created your heart first
Within it
A bright
That could not be tarnished
Even by abiding hands
A glow that could not be dimmed
Even by the darkest night....

A Reckless Faller

I am reckless faller
Dependent on the weak catcher
Is it a surprise that I crash with a loud thud
That the blood from my nostrils reminds me of burning
That the bones have cracked out from my skin
That my insides have splattered into a sour song
The sidewalk held me against its hardened heart and spoke to me
A man will love you with lies
But I will kill you with truth
I died there on the concrete
Because I believed in man
And my death was a reminder of his failures

The Birth of a New Legend

Wait for me
And I for you
We'll walk on water
Or on a sea departed
Take my hand
As we stand
Hidden amongst a field of yellow weeds
Beside them we'll live
Together we'll grow
The cicadas will sing our names
The fireflies will intertwine
As they give light to our light
We'll love beneath a canopy of leaves
We'll roam alongside the century old trees
Our feet have touched the forest floor
The clouds have parted
And the pink sunset remains
Let God make legend of our union

The Unwanted

Over the landmines I ran
Though I sank amongst the sinking
sand
Diving into the acidic sea
Burning with a drowning plea
Do you not wish for me?

Dizzy with a transparent blue
The yellow-eyed fish gave light a
clue
The mirror of the moonlight's
reflections
Against the deep sea's interpretation
Somehow led me here to you

Though you hid beneath the rocky
cracks
They screamed to me of your wicked
tracks
Fearful and fragile you lay
With our union came a decomposing
decay
Was there nothing more to you?

How disappointing the weak can be
Watching the fleeting flee
My naive mind birthed a hopeful dream
But it was no more than a dreamer's scheme

The Wait Part 1

Wait
For the last ice
The final knife to crash into me
Its last shattering words
Left to melt into my silence
Wait
For the dying leaf
Brown with grief
Already fallen to its last breath
Asleep in death
Pour your sorrow into me
Wait
For the cold breeze
Blow past my chilling heart
Until the air gives out
Come take my frozen breathe away
Wait
For the broken branch
Crooked and cracked as it may
Fall to the unknowing ground
Becoming nothing more but a useless thing
Wait
For the open sky
To close its university of light
And swallow up the beautiful
Leaving me here in the dark
Wait

For the ticking of time
As it never sleeps
You tell me to wait forever
But I cannot do that
Wait
For the man who knows not of waiting
His voice a sound of echoes
Lingering like ghosts to follow
Leading me to the lost

The Wait Part 2

Should I choose hunger
Perched up against your indecisive air
Forever bound by the glare of your stare
Here in this quiet
Starving to be saved
A fairytale princess behaved
Sleeping amongst captivity
Though there are no chains
No locks but the daunting pains
That a prince remains
Would you come for me then
In the wait of waiting
Or merely from afar, watch me to end
In the fade of fading

Private Caller

You throw hate at me
But it never really comes back to you
Because the phone rings
And I hear your voice again
Hidden behind your sarcasm
Peeking through your curiosity
Is the real reason why you called
I know you still love me
Trying to put an ocean between us
But I still feel your breath on me
Your voice in front of mine
As if it's always been there
That bittersweet tone makes me laugh anyway
Talking with an offensive ease
Like you didn't want to speak to me
So tell me this love:
Why did you call?

What They Say

They say **all you need is a good man!**
I wish I could see this as true.
They say **get you a rich man!**
If only I could say this and this be true.
They say **a man is better than no man at all!**

Is that right?

A good man can hold my heart but the right one can wear it.
It could fit so perfectly and look like his own
Because it was made for him.
A good man who holds my heart has the potential to drop it.

Does fresh food not spoil?
Does everything known to be good stay good?
But a man who wears my heart can't drop it.
Nor would he risk breaking it.

Can a man lose a heart if he wears it as his own?
A rich man can buy my heart but the right one searched for my heart.
Does a man who buys a heart care more about the cost or the heart?

A man made out of money is money who made a man.

If a man lost all his money, wouldn't he be willing to sell a heart?

If it was all he had, his last possession, in the name of money

Didn't he already sell his own?

If money gave birth to him and he birth money, will he not be devoted to what he has bore?

My heart cannot compete with a man's soul-child!

A Lesson About Snakes

Beautiful snake, slither away
Your intentions are never too kind
You patronize me with your elegant dance
Suddenly I'm hypnotized

You entice me with your black eyes
Now I've fallen into a deep trance
My eyes follow yours as we go back and forth
You make a mockery of me before the townspeople
They laugh at me pointing and shouting
The silly girl who was tricked by the snake
I was under your spell

So you decided to take your time
You wrapped your body around mine
We became intertwined
You glided all over me
You had your way with me until you were satisfied
As you unraveled yourself away from me

It was time to decide your fate for me
As you kept my eyes on yours
You let yourself into my soul
Seeing a helpless child who thought
Snakes to be beautiful
One foolish enough to get close to one
You scolded me with your eyes
Calling me a stupid girl

"Don't you know snakes are dangerous?

Everyone knows not come near us."
You hissed
For a moment you felt sorry
For me as your eyes softened
For a second I thought your compassion
Would free me.

"Compassion is not enough."
And just like that
With one quick movement
He struck me dead

Sing To Me___________

Beneath the loud
siren of your
breath
A sweeter sound
rings___________________
Sing to me a
lover's death
As a king to his
queen
Set aglow your
eyes for me
And I shall know
light___________________
Give me your soul
that I might
finally see
More than this
night you fight to
be______________________

Pretty Green Eyes

What eyes you have
And the beauty they exude
Are you unaware of how they shine
As the sun confides in them
As green as a blade of grass
On a bright noon day
Are you unfamiliar with the golden rays
Your eyes betray
The color still ripe from your youth
Your eyes could taste of green apples
Fresh and crisp from the street market
Though you seem troubled
Your face tells a story your eyes can hide
Pretending you don't live a life of crime
But those eyes are fighting for peace
Looking for purity and innocence
How odd you look
With a rough body yet kind eyes
Green leaves
Those pretty green eyes
Its hard for me not to gaze by
And roam to find all the treasures that rest
inside
Those pretty green eyes....

Together Never Again

With your broken eyes
Look at me completely
I've consumed you half alive
But there you stare at me
The glare of a sweet empty
Awaiting my love still
But now I am thirsty
Would you not give me a heart fulfilled
Standing with a hostile courtesy
Touch my soul if it be your will
But your air like a lonely sea
And all I'll ever know is but the cold of your chill

Poets' Block

Poetically frozen
Corroded beneath the blinding white
No words but the breath
Of a cold cloud I uttered
An airy dust
Freed from my lips
While the blood of silence
Poured on the carpet of snow
Lost in the speechless winter
Until the ice confided in me
Conversing in a muted language
Occasionally frostbitten
By its captivating tongue
Bound by the confines of a Poets' Block
Even the light
Seared its bright fire
Into my hypothermic thought
My fingers too fried to write
I melted into its fears
Until I am but numb
To the words I once was

Telling Time

Come now time
With your bittersweet sublime
Lift from me, your vengeance spell
And wish me well
This journey I am on
And let me awake to a radiant dawn
What have I done
That you collapsed the unwilling sun
Awakening
The roaring of the churning cloud
The whistling winds screaming aloud
Nature I fear
Lacking of sweet cheer
Birth forth a great storm on me
Its fury laid out for all to see
Fallen on bended knee
To time I plead

Let me be

Moth

You touched me
And set my shoulder ablaze
Though it was not your hand
That created the fire
But the words you spoke to me
I could not put out
So there I sat
Burning up in your words
Like a moth to a flame

Best Friend

Could your success tear me away?
Would my failure obey?
A friendship departed,
A loss regarded,
Are we to be
A separated sea?
I would think not
We a ship rot;
For you are my dearest one,
As a mother to her begotten son.

A House Is Not A Home

Should I make a bed out of shame,
And a blanket the same?
What good could I be,
The undertaking of a solitary me,
To rest my soul night after night,
Lying in a disturbed delight—
A house full of sorrow
Built for no tomorrows?
Why, that's no way to live;
Only death it gives.

ZOMBIE

The intrigue of pretty green
Makes the saliva runneth over
The thirst lingers until we are all mad with it
Our spirit laid to rest
The dead swallow our hidden dreams
For their ancestors did the same
Awake child
Open your reckless eyes and take notice upon yourself
See what a spectacle you have become
To die and be resurrected
But look, you are still dead
Only you are just a vessel
Filled with nothingness
Just an empty pity
Standing hopelessly like a dumb carcass

On that assembly line
Dying for your turn at your precious zombie's chocolate
The hunger stinging your throat
Like needles scratching
Going only where the blood runs
Immersed in debt and bills
Our bodies have long gave way
Such weary fragile shells
But the will to suffer on quietly continues
The body has no other choice but to function
With our decrepit feet
We'll walk until out toes fall off
All in the name of those dead presidents
We'll all chase after it
Until the bullet forges its way through our head

Middle Class

To many of us
Our jobs are like burning flesh
Upon our own skin
A slow torture
To become content with
Though the screaming calms
And the body numbs
It is then you wonder
When did we all become comfortable
dying like this?

Red Line

I was on the train
When all the white people got off
Sox-35th
The last stop before fear
Turning a certain shade of freedom
They walked off with a safe ease
Looking at us inside the car
And I knew those eyes
For I had seen them before
Watching us like we were cattle
Being sent to a slaughter
And for a moment I hated them
Because they would never know that feeling

There Are...

There are big extravagant churches
Sitting in the middle of the ghettos
Like a prized mantel piece in a dirty
room.
How much worth can that mantel piece
serve
If it cannot shine beauty to the rest of
the room?
There are black women,
Naked and tired,
Pregnant and sexy.
With nowhere to go
But in the black man's eye.
It is only sad when it's the only place
she goes
Because there too are dreams
For the black woman to have
And there too are places
The black woman should see.
There are black men,
Young and foolish,
Who don't understand
Why their pants should not sag,
Or why their hair should not be messy,
Or why their tongue should not always
be aggressive,
Who lack understanding
That a society has judged them
And found them guilty.
The young black man
Says he doesn't care,
Marked in tattoos,
Rough and wild,
Content in his ignorance,
Sizzling in the heat,
With a constant sweat in his eye–

FOREVER KNOWN AS A THREAT,
LABELED AN ETERNAL TROUBLE:
A SPECIMEN
UNDER A PERMANENT MICROSCOPE,
ALWAYS UNDER WATCH,
ALWAYS FEARED.

THERE ARE BLACK MEN,
GIFTED YET UNINSPIRED,
ENTREPRENEURS YET SELLERS OF WATER.
THERE ARE BLACK MEN,
YOUNG AND OLD,
AND ALL OF THEM BEAUTIFUL,
WHO ARE MISUNDERSTOOD.

THE BLACK MAN CALLS ME A QUEEN;
THE BLACK MAN ALWAYS LETS ME ON THE BUS FIRST;
THE BLACK MAN LAUGHS WITH AN EFFORTLESS EASE;
THE BLACK MAN TALK IS WELCOMING;
THERE IS SO MUCH THAT IS GREAT ABOUT A BLACK MAN,
BUT THEIR LACK OF EFFORT TO SHOW THE WORLD
WHO THEY REALLY ARE
IS THE SADDEST PART.

THERE ARE BLACK PEOPLE
TOO ANGRY AT A FUTURE
THEY CAN CHANGE,
BUT TOO WEARY TO TRY—
INSTEAD REMAIN FIRMLY ATTACHED TO THE PUPPET MASTER
WHO PLAYS THE STRINGS,
WHICH NO ONE WILL CUT,
JUST MERELY DANCE TO THE SONG HE SINGS.

Judgment Day

A part of me wants to run
As far as I can
Away from this city
That's set on fire
But the other part of me
Wants to catch me if I can
And put out
The wild fire
That's burning them alive
Not knowing how to die
They suffer slowly
And it stings my eyes
To watch this unconscious chaos
In permanent pause
And the ones who care
Are poor too
While the other ones
Just line 'em up
And watch them burn

God give me the strength
To set this city on water
And submerge its thirst in the cool
And wash away the demons' heat
And blow away the devil's air
In the depth of the sea;

Baptize the human thought
And calm the flames
While the wrenching of the waves
Knock against the unenlightened
fighter
And tug at their souls
Which beg them to rise.

Ascension

I'm ascending...
Floating above into some heavenly place
Loosed from the burdens that consumed me
From below the evils of life are mere ants to me
My emancipation is written within the clouds
(The sky still astounding
Endless still)
Some overlapping
Creating images amongst themselves...

What I would give to halt time
To stop this plane and leap unthinkingly
Allured by these massive cotton-like bodies
And whichever cloud I landed upon
Would catch me like a ball into a glove
And caress me with its fluffy translucent fingers

I imagine there is a hidden world
Between the earth and heaven
I would walk cloud to cloud until I found the secret city
And there I would stay all the day long
Melted between the sweet cotton candy clouds
As the wind carried me softly by and by

Moon

Take notice upon the moon,
Hanging effortlessly,
Lacking strings to hold its place.
Above me, it glows from the freedom it is given.
Jealousy is all I feel.
Here I am bound,
With endless rules,
Moving only by the conditions of control.
I have no will of my own,
Fulfilling desires that are not entirely my own.
Even while I drive, it is because I must.
The world has become more of a burden than a
happiness.
O moon,
Help me:
I follow you yet cannot reach you,
But there you are,
Never too far that I cannot see you.
Is it your wish to torment me?
To expose your carefree face,
Upon my tired soul?
Tonight you light yourself a more fluorescent color,
Turning a shade yellow,
Like a lamp from inside a window,
I see no shadows lurking inside you.
Perhaps you are just as lonely as I am,
For there is a vacancy within you
That possibly I could fill—
The woman inside the moon.
I could be as free as you;
I would revel in it.
Only you run when I run to you,
Though you appear frighteningly still.
Moon, do not fear me.

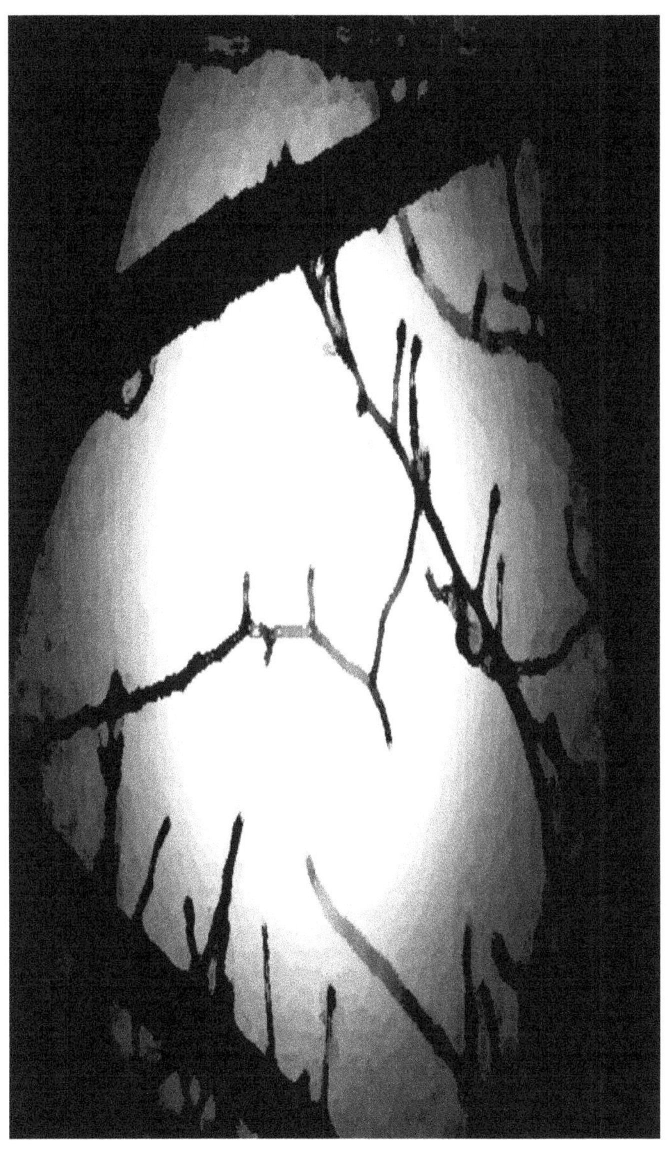

The Unknown

There are places flashlights have never entered or lanterns never lit
The fog writes my name through the air
It has no voice to call my name
The echoes of past lives whisper to me to find what remains but are far hidden
Now their ashes scatter on unseen places
Wishing a mortal eye could witness such a sight
They call but on deaf ears it falls
They lie within the mountains and caves
Awaiting sound ears to hear their cryptic code that flows softly in the wind
I hear them in the distance
Where they are I am not prepared to go
Still I am afraid but longing for a dark beauty
There is so much to see sealed in the deep black crevices of the earth
Only the dead have seen the true value of the dirt we walk on
Before the sun vanishes leaving its trail of light to the night
The sky dresses in a midnight blue
A mirror reflecting the sea
With just enough light to guide me into the unknown
I walk on
Lured into the depths of shadows
I am bound by fear
Nonetheless my body functions fearlessly
Fulfilling my curiosity is the only cure
To rid my permanent suspicion of the unknown

Sun Kiss

The Orange warmth
Reaching out
With golden touches
Pink breath
And purple
whispers
Ambiance
Filled above
A private love
Exposed above us
Color consumed clouds
Keep floating
Keep roaming
The sky is maddened
with life
Its blue churning
Making
anew
More colors
Until the sun sets
And the kiss
Is over

Today

Today I am choosing to live my happy ending
Beginning with smelling the scent of a new day
The sky is so innocent
Waiting for me to attend to it
The air is sweeter than the day before
My troubles lifted from me
As the wind blows them away
The wind is so clever sometimes
Sweeping me off my feet with its freshness
Lifting me so high above the burdens that cannot reach me
Knocking life right into me
I find myself floating
On endless tomorrows
And forever thereafter
The sun wraps me in its blanket of warmth
Scorching away the sorrows that chase me
Protecting me from the past and the reminders it brings –
The power in a new day is miraculous
Deleting yesterday
Not allowing it to deteriorate today
It colors a black and white society with bright vibrant colors…

Church

The air
My favorite dessert
Laid right beneath my nose
As I consumed its sweetness
It blew a peace
I remembered before
And I was comforted
For it was merely God
Blowing me a kiss again
Blushing with color
The stained glass windows
And waiting to be seen
Finally
Pressed against it
A light
Peering through to me
It was God's eyes
Watching the dance
And the aroma of worship
Decorated and scented
Lifted itself
And headed towards God
His nose savored the smell
Then dressed in a smile
There was a sudden glory surrounded in our midst
As we dined in heaven
In the purity of infiniteness

The Fire

What becomes of the lost
Those unable to find rest
Yet moving constantly
Wondering aimlessly through life
Finding contentment in nothing

Resilient roamers we have become
As the earth's dust
Settles uncomfortably
Beneath our feet
Afraid to cling on
To this dangerous journey
We tread upon

Into the depths of nowhere
And a place of constant dark
Our eyes too black
To see the path God gave us

Our limbs function
But only to the will of fear
Moving accordingly
Finding nowhere to lay our head
Walking because we are alive
But it is clear we are dead

Succumbing to an evil
Who in perfect timing
Presented a devilish smile

Indulged in the distraction
We wondered with a blind approval
Into the dark of the woods
And bathed in the poison ivy
Living lavishly as the forgotten
Traveling deeper and further

Into the realms of chaos
We thought we left behind

The devil is clever
Offering an easy way out
When in essence
Taking you right to hell

As the flames begin
And death in front of us
It is exactly in this moment
We decide if we survive

Shall we forfeit
The power God has given us
Do we sink beneath the fire
Or shall we rise above the flame

Why should we act
As if we are already ash
When the fire has barely burned us
With one call to Jesus
To tell this fire to cease
Would the fire not cease

With just his name
Resurrected from our mouth
Would his presence not come
In the form of a waterfall
Would his voice not come
In the form of a cool breeze

Just that name would provoke a sanity
That no fire could tame
Even though the fire still rises
It is far more important
For God to save your mind
In the confines of hell

Rather than extinguish the hell
And save you last
He shows you that with him
You can survive the impossible
With him
The impossible is made possible

Divinity

God is divine
The way he brought you to me
Without so much as a warning
As he placed you before me
Before me you sat unrecognizable
Unimaginable to my mind
You were just another man
Like the ones seated next to you
Suddenly God intervened
And made you so much more to me
At that moment
You were no longer camouflaged
With the many men surrounding you
You filled my eyes with your colors
The way a rainbow paints across
A dull gray sky
You became the only reason to see
No one else mattered
They were saturated with black and white
Never to stand out and illuminate my sight
But your reds and yellows were blinding
Could you be more beautiful
God is divine
How does he decide who will connect with who
And who will feel for who

Maybe it is not for you and I to know
But it is amazing
To have no control
And watch God create magic
Between you and a complete stranger

I Remember I Forgot You

You stood there so casually
With a brilliant sort of smile
Your eyes look like the saving kind
Rescue me from myself
Because my heart has lost its feeling
I'm waiting to hear its pulsating rhythms again
Its silence deafening
It's so much more painful not to feel
I'd look forward to the spoils of heartbreak and loves lost
Just so my heart could be a part of something
To know more than this motionless and frighteningly still
Organ she has taken on
You stand there frozen
Talking as if time stood still
Look beyond my admiring face
Inside I have fallen apart
Behind my kind eyes
Is an urgency crying out
Waiting for your hands to crawl
Outside your pockets
And draw near to me
Every meeting between us becomes less urgent
And I haven't felt this way in so long

Don't send me back into that lonely sea
Where even the waves no longer find me
I'm surrounded by an endless calm
"I hope I see you again."
You always say
The taste too bitter to savor
Each word used as a tool of torture
Knocking my limbs every which way
Until I am but a pile of unorganized body parts
Broken
Unfit to be put back together again
You walk swiftly
Unconcerned of our fate
Just joyous of our reunion
You have been one man
That has awakened me from such a dull, visionless sleep
A present of possibilities you proposed to me
Surprising my view with a bouquet of love and lust
It's been so long since anyone gave me flowers
Hope wasn't just an invisible dream
I was beginning to see the ripples of promise
Maybe you and I were never to be
But just the thought I needed to believe

Girl Meets World

As soon as you go inside of me
I'm unplugged from the rest of the world
Nothing even matters
But your breath on mine
I'm thrown into morning
As my body awakes from a dreamer's death
Resurrected by the early dew
And the aroma of earth
My suspicion of being alive
Unveils itself at that moment
My disoriented mind is sober again
And I take in the day
Outside the window
There is life waiting for me
A force pulling at me to move
Onward from this dark lit room
Next to me he slumbers
Like the night still owned the sky
Sifting through his dreams
As a character in its play
He looks peaceful but his body lays reckless
I look at him wondering

If he is as fond of me as he claims
Or am I just a body to sleep next to
A voice to talk to
I wish in his lifeless body
His lips would move me
With truth
With words of adoration
Or even spite
Anything to set my uncertain
Mind at ease
But he is only a man
I make a note to myself
As I look at him once more
I will not fall deeply for him
I fear one day he would
Betray my heart and leave it
For dead
I look through the window
And I'm reminded
That is where I ought to be

Chance At Love

If only the mouth
would speak
And un-kept
promises believe
Would I seek the lips
of a man
A mouth that will not
say
What the eyes convey
But who has the
ability to decode the
code of eyes

All that I can

decipher

Is the fighter

Who battles with the

pride of lies

Men with their

frozen mouths

Burn until the truth

spills out

And maybe

Just maybe

You'll have a chance

at love

Fear

I fear not
In a love
Not existing
But the birthing pains
Of broken heartedness
Conceived
And the grievances born
That see to it
My reason for being
Be my end
Birth from my soul
My soul mate
Unspeakable sorrow
For tomorrow he should die
Thus I fear
To bear witness
Of a love divided
Never to mend
Itself again
My heart is fragile
Unwilling to beat
Against such unruly schemes
I would come undone
Torn at the seams
And to all who saw me
I was nothing but a sufferer
For all the days
Of my life
I fear not
In loneliness
For it knows
No such hurts
But of quiet and silence
But I fear love

For its many attacks
On a weakened soul
Without a moment's hesitation
I will say it
I do not fear to be unloved
But oh how I fear to be loved

I Love You

I loved him because he loved me
Without reason
But that our skin the same
And if not
Then a beautiful stranger
That I'd be striking to him
With no knowledge
Of whom I truly am
Still
I love you came
With an outpouring
A knowing
With no common language we shared
But a silent smile
And an unknown laughter
He loved me still
And "I love you" rained
Our love remained
Without question
For my love he fought
And won viciously
With his enemies
Spoiled beneath his foot
A trophy of hearts
Ripped out of the very men departed
Held victoriously in his hands
He stood like a conqueror
For my love he'd die
No need for a name

Or the substance that filled me in-between
My face was his dream

Mi morena
Save your ring finger
It's mine....
Te amo mi amor
Un beso para Luis
I love you

I thought I would be different

I thought I would be different
I thought I would be the one to tell that tall tale of true love still existing
Still persisting its way through my heart

I thought I would find it
I thought I would be the one to see love hidden beneath the dusted ashes and cobwebs
Entrapped in a place too dark for others to see but unto my eyes it would beautifully be

I thought I would feel it
I thought I would be the one to feel more than momentary and beyond temporary pleasure
love that had stability undeviating,
Unrelenting love that grew past a pipe dream and wasn't just a hype dream but it was a story of my life dream

I thought I would be different
I thought I would be the one to touch what my mind told my fingers was love
Grazing my hands on a feeling so rich and smooth, surging a tingling sensation that interrupted my senses causing my mind to panic because real love was never discovered and defined until I touched it.

I thought I would know it
I thought I would be the one to distinguish
it from the imitations that pretend be love
That never really see love
That I would reach the pinnacle of joy
That I would reach the culmination of
happiness fulfilled by this thing called love

I thought I would know it like the night
knows the glow of the white moon

I thought I would know it like the North
Star knows to lead the misguided

I thought I would understand it

I thought I would be the one to write
countless books filled with words love had
not yet described because many would not
know it

I thought I would be different
I thought love would test me
Volunteer my heart
Experimental sessions of love lessons
Learning how to bore my heart of fruitful
blossoms that nourished it
And I would know how to take proper care
of it

Not tearing it by carelessly sharing it with
people who could care less of it

I thought I would be love's patient
Taking under surgery to heal these wounded
scars by impersonators that claimed to be
love where then I would be restored by real
love and nursed into a miraculous vision

I thought I would be different
But I am just the same as you
Hoping that I will have love in its purity
When it is authentic and genuine
Waiting until it surfaces itself true

I will not give up on love

I will be different

Discovery

Bound within my skin
Softened by the cushions of love
Spacious eternity
Wherein lies
A **yearning** to be breached
To **break down** the walls of hesitancy
Tear down the veins of fear
Words framed in a perfect picture
Lunge from my lips
And **echo** throughout the hills
In need of a rare man
With a profound tone
To **project** a pure truth to me
To **ripple** a sound I adore
And **shut down** my prideful movement
So that **I may open** up to him
And **he may discover** me

Night

I walk with pride and with every stride
I walk with invincibility
No fear just the spear in my eyes piercing
The night as if I claimed it
And made it surrender to me

I carry the night on my back
Lifting every worried and cautious movement
That keeps me, grabs me, and holds me under
There is something about the night air that
owns us
And the sound of footsteps puts my mind into
a frenzy
And I become dizzy to my surroundings

Losing the war to my self-declaration that says
I should feel safe
Instead the eerie noises of gates whistling,
signs shaking, and unwelcoming shadows
follow me like unwanted guests
I was not going to be made an innocent victim
of the night
That acted like a shameless bully

The further I walked, the streets became
scarcer, and the street paths became narrower
until I found myself walking through
alleyways

The streetlights flickering, ticking their last
beats of light
Timing my demise into the shell of complete
darkness
The trees waving in the wind, warning me to
turn around from what lies ahead

But I walk on and I walk alone
Like a lone soldier
Awaiting uncertainty
Knowing the lines of life and death have
become blurred
I am that soldier, the one who is unafraid to die

I march on through the night
Feeling like I have something to prove
That I can walk alone
Like brave warriors on the frontline of the
battlefield
Like a reckless roamer who abandoned the exit
signs and escape routes

I was facing the night head on
Competing against its game
I was not going to get played by night
I was now playing alongside
Not surrendering to the whims of its
frightening appearance

Instead I decorate my face
Like that of a medieval knight

Riding on my headless horsemen
Into the legends of its midnight nightmares
Preparing for a battle my mind had already
won
The night will not win
I will not be afraid

Yet there are eyes lurking like fireflies waiting
for the perfect moment to strike
Or the imprinted dark traces of bodies
watching me from afar
Hoping to catch me when no one is looking
It is the sound of steps so close behind me
The thumping of drums beating
And the pounding of panic
That gnaws at my courage

The night used to be so beautiful and calm
Known for its late night walks underneath its
dark nakedness
Revealing its beauty mark of stars
That left permanent traces of where it begins
and never ends
Glowing its moon like face upon me
So I could take notice on it and enjoy what
night is

When did it abandon us?
Did it make a deal with the devil?
Turning it over to the wicked that use the night
as a playground to keep us from it

We find a way to live our lives and make it home before five
Did the night conspire with the evil doers?

I can no longer walk alone
A body I cannot recognize interrupts my space
I see a knife and I can no longer see a face
But a knife and I freeze
With the inability to move or think
And I realize all efforts to prove that I am unhindered and unshakeable
Have been tarnished in mere seconds

Everything I worked so hard to build has shattered
Predicting ten thousand episodes of how the scene should end almost makes me ill
All I can do is breathe my first breath I waited so long to breathe knowing it could have been my last
The realization sinks in that nothing can prepare you
For the night

Déjà vu

The night is too still
And the air too calm
The streets too bare
The people too quiet
Our movement too ordinary
Our dress too plain
Our thoughts too similar
Our paths are too the same
Did God forget about us
Are we a page unwritten
Where has our story gone
God where is our tomorrow
Is it to be just like today
Is everything to be as expected
Moving without surprise
Have we been put with the forgotten
Left to fend for ourselves
Without the glory of God
He who makes ripe things sweet
And sweet things sweeter
I am here living
Yet not witnessing the vision of chaos
All under the same moon
The swelling of colored laughter in the air
The swoon of undertones sung
I am here living
Yet lacking the sight of some lively thing
So out of my window
I stare into the
Dark shadowy places
Hoping that magic lives inside them
I am here living
Yet not really living at all

~~Déjà vu~~

~~The night is too still~~
~~And the air too calm~~
~~The streets too bare~~
~~The people too quiet~~
~~Our movement too ordinary~~
~~Our dress too plain~~
~~Our thoughts too similar~~
~~Our paths are too the same~~
~~Did God forget about us~~
~~Are we a page unwritten~~
~~Where has our story gone~~
~~God where is our tomorrow~~
~~Is it to be just like today~~
~~Is everything to be as expected~~
~~Moving without surprise~~
~~Have we been put with the forgotten~~
~~Left to fend for ourselves~~
~~Without the glory of God~~
~~He who makes ripe things sweet~~
~~And sweet things sweeter~~
~~I am here living~~
~~Yet not witnessing the vision of chaos~~
~~All under the same moon~~
~~The swelling of colored laughter in the air~~
~~The swoon of undertones sung~~
~~I am here living~~
~~Yet lacking the sight of some lively thing~~
~~So out of my window~~
~~I stare into the~~
~~Dark shadowy places~~
~~Hoping that magic lives inside them~~
~~I am here living~~
~~Yet not really living at al~~

Troy.

Troy was a mythical place
Too magical to be overtaken
Too hidden to be found by outsiders
It was too special to be overcrowded

That was why I could still hear
The crickets chirp at night
Demanding their song to be heard
Singing a broken chorus
Their croaking like violent violin strings

At times I would hate them
And other times comforting
The way their voices floated from the ground
Natural and beautiful
The traffic played to my ears
Creating a sound harmonious
A lullaby I slept to
A symphony of horns and engines
Humming its rioted tune

The night was more welcoming than the day
Never uncovering an intimidating or frightening
face
That can be so ever-present in big cities

In Troy
The night had taken on a compassionate dark
Accepting all that found its black appealing
It became a haven where people
And animals come to dance underneath the stars
And as it lit the sky
And fireflies flickered like strobe lights

Time seemed to stand still

Perfection
A sight rarely seen
Almost considered non existent
Would rise occasionally from its
Secret places and find rest there

When It Comes...

What spies at me from
Beyond these city limits
Already the echo of screams
Scratching at my throat
Movement so swift
The shadows
As thick as thieves
Ready to steal my innocence
Rid my naïve mind
Of thoughts dreamt in fairytales
Like mad men
Their saliva runs
In sloppy drops
Their busy hands
Hurry over one another
Too crazed to keep them still
Their schizophrenic eyes
Bloodshot from want
Shake back and forth
Envisioning my demise
Lions have roared
This warning before
They have come to consume
Towns like mine
Its purity a delicacy
Their corruption
Is deadly
They've killed millions
And turned thousands
Into the likes of them
My town was one of the

Last few towns left
And now they hunt for us
They stay hidden in the darkness
Lurking like yellow-eyed wolves
In need of devouring
The good that still remains
The world is becoming
A scary place
Soon I fear
Even the small towns
Will not be safe

City Love

Isolated from a perfect picture
I stalked his grand museum
A beauty denied to my flesh
Only with my adoring eyes
Could I search his naked luxury
Craving his handsome charm
From a distant gray highway
I gazed at the sky scrapers
Draped exquisitely in fluorescent lighting
Like Christmas Day
A victorious array of buildings stood
Reaching towards the sky
(As to conquer her I'm not for sure)
Once a defiled collage
And unorganized metal
Reinvents itself
In ode to him
A vision frozen
A Mona Lisa smile
Standing in the heart of the city
His gladiator stance
Lacking a welcoming appeal
But his purpose did excite
The mind of the lonely and lost
To entertain the lacking
The small-towners in need of more
To those who traveled
From near and far
for a spectacle
Like downtown nights

Relocation
TIMES
HSBC
SAMSUNG
YOGA
JUNE 21

In Africa

In Africa
I would let my hair down
Because I knew the wind
Would rummage through it
Blowing centuries of history
Right past my neck
I was in the land
I had always heard about
But a land I've never known
But as soon as the wind
Tossed my hair into a reverie
I knew her then

In Africa
I would wear skirts and dresses
Back home
I would look forward to death
Than dress like that
But in Africa
I wore many
Because I knew the wind
Could make them dance
Flinging my clothes wherever she desired
She made me fly

In Africa
I would wear bright clothes
Black and white failed to find me
Instead the colors followed me
I wanted to shine like the sun
That hovered over me

Impress her with my colors
From then on she would walk with me
Together we lit our paths
Talking for hours on end
Enticed by her thoughtfulness
Hypnotized by her playfulness

Africa would spend all afternoon with me
There we were
Slow dancing in the wind

A Work of Art

Today, we are just a memory to one another,
One that is surely to fade,
Where it will find rest with the lost,
And never to resurface its perfection ever again.
The paths we tread upon,
Have led us further astray,
Until the distance between us overcomes me.
I have no other choice but to walk with the forgotten,
But I refuse to let this disease of my mind ail me.
I will find a way of remembrance.
For fate rarely unravels such a gift as this,
To find a home in such a far away place.
Moments created in time too miraculous to give up.
God made each one of us,
Like that of a jagged, unattended puzzle piece
Never showing Himself more apparent
When brought together,
Our pieces fell next to each other.
Without force and connected
No longer a puzzle but canvas,
Into a reverie,
Are colors ran so,
Creating somewhat of a masterpiece.

Four Month Love

Four Month Love/It was your smile that touched me first/That grin could put a twinkle/Inside the uneven devil's eye/You laughed and it lit/The ever clouded sky/You were easy to love/My four month love/You held me in your eyes/The way night clung to/Its star in the darken sky/We were inseparable
Unable to find contentment/With anyone else
You were the key to Africa/Together we unlocked her forgotten past/Together we found her infinite joys

A Letter To Africa

Africa, remember me,
Because you live in my dreams, you see,
And you persistently rest there.
Reminding me of your dark stare
You roam through my mind stretching as far
and as vast as your land.
Like a familiar stranger
I stepped on your land for the first time,
And the earth rumbled a roar,
Awakening for my arrival,
A celebration,
An initiation,
And I felt your love.
You sent your native greeters to show me your
humble beginnings and never-endings.
The thought of leaving you –
My eyes would deny my tears such truth.
Unbelieving, the cry would come anyway,
Like a serene fall on your driest desert,
An untroubled waterfall into your Zimbabwe
rivers.
Ngiyakuthanda:
A confession of my love to you
In a language you gave birth to,
A language I'm proud to speak to you.
I honor you
For your endurance because you still remain,
Untarnished and untainted,
But revitalized after perpetual abuses,

Baptized from the sin of theft and
abandonment,
Of war and famine,
Corruption,
Frequent destruction.
You still remain.
The trees still stand strong and firmly rooted
Nor loosing the color of a deep dark green.
The valleys have not yet crumbled;
Instead, remain carved as a record of obstacles
that will not deter them.
The mountains have not yet collapsed,
But stand as watchtowers that protect the land
of Africa.
Your oceans and rivers have not yet dried
But pierce the land with power to quench a
land that will never thirst,
Because even the rains still fall abundantly on
Africa,
A downpour of blessings.
But only the wise man understands
It is not the dealings of silver and gold
But the internal sustenance of an incomparable
soul,
A secret dwelling of a love divine,
That is unobtainable unless given by the Lord
our God.
An evil mind could never identify such an
importance.

Africa, your fury should burn for the
misfortune you have been given from others
who didn't know you.
You still did not shield or hide your beauty
But have given it to all who wishes to witness
your splendor.
Even the very shape of your land commands
attention as a wonder of the world .
You could never be ignored nor could you ever
be forgotten.
You are a picture that cannot be painted by
mortal hands.
You are words that cannot be described or
uttered by human mouth.

Mama Africa, you are a mother that cannot be
replaced.

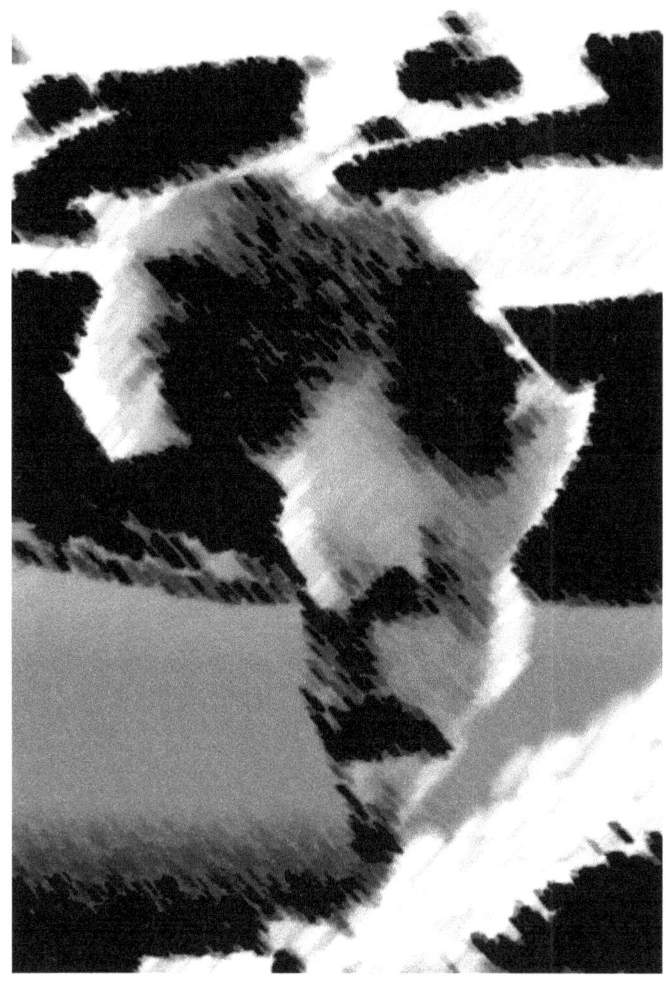

Africa Part 1

This surface I can no longer walk on
My feet dance clumsily to this unheard song
Stumbling over yet another
Of its troubling questions
Until I have but fallen into wonderment,
And there the unspeakable went
An untellable wise
For my reckless eyes
Hungry for the allure
And suddenly I crave her
Before me a goddess
Undressed in a naked serenity,
I envy her, her eternity
She is rough looking
Though not mean
For her purity is what her skin is made out of
As she was conceived by the superior; which could only be that of love
No one eye could misplace her shape
Nor could any man disturb an unshakable fate
For even her imperfections are striking.
As it was so, she was created a queen for the unruly king
Her pride has never failed her
She speaks in a language only the wind knows
Her voice but a whisper
Her song, her spiritual sister
She rests inside the core of your heart
Beating life inside death, love she thwart

Africa Part 2

Like a river wild
She's consumed you
Taking you deeper than any other place in the world;
Sweeping you through the mountains where the ancestors roam,
Where you hear the Zulus shouting in an exalted moan,
Devoted to the tribal dances inherited from generations past,
For every dance shall be as the last
Transforming the legs of the young,
Moving in rhythms that unite a Zulu nation,
The feet and drums are one in the same,
With the praises came the ancestral rain
Spilling throughout the valleys and into the villages,
The Zulu men, like Shaka's warriors, wrapped in fur cloth,
Standing tall with a shield in one hand and the spear in the other.
The Zulu women adorned in beaded jewelry,
Covered only with color over their lively breasts
And around the carving of their hips
While headpieces so lavishly
Display an appearance of a wilderness royalty
Laughter and singing own the air with a sweet sense of tradition;
A sweet sense of South Africa.
But she is also the shack-like homes which barely stand,
She is also in the poor lone man
She is where rooms are scarcely limited;
Where space is all too lacking,
And the children who are barefoot
And there she is resting inside the African red soot
But the wind speaks
Tenderly talking to the bright colored clothes that sway from the lines,
As the sun favors this place because she glows a triumphant grin just then.

And it is known that there is even beauty in Africa's pain and suffering;
In the harshness she is often given,
There is a constant eye that never leaves her;
Even though foreigners extract her treasures,
And commoners trample on her fortunes
Her value is more than riches and comes not by money
But from her land who is faithful to endurance remaining self- sustaining ,
And from her people that refuse to die but will always live on.

Poetry Africa

I was Alice
And Africa my Wonderland
I had only scratched the surface of the forest floor
Before the most brilliant fall came upon me
Beyond the schoolyard
Past the flat crown trees
Further beyond where the monkeys roamed
Deeper into the green that surrounded me
Were words
Like smoke from a chimney
I had been led by Africa's words
If you listened closely
You could hear their echoes from the window

For a moment I was Alice
Thinking with the same curious mind
To seek out what no one else would find
The forgotten ones
The young ones
All speaking directly to her
Africa herself
Her bloodline
Echoing her thoughts

These words became my link to Africa
Her truth
My oxygen
These poetic writers
Fused the air with words that spoke to my heart
It was the breathe of life
The taste just as sweet
Nothing mattered but her words
Every Tuesday after class
I ran away to follow her words
Just so I could touch Africa a moment more

With every cry they whimpered
With every celebrative shout they sang
I was with them
Taken by her words
Suddenly I was Alice no more
I became the makeup that was Wonderland
I was no longer the foreigner
I no longer needed a name

Before Africa

Before Africa,
Snow was beautiful to me.
I was always overcome by it.
The brightness of it, demanding you to attend to it,
Take notice upon it and admire its white.
A color that strong,
You could rarely appreciate any other beauty,
Especially any that sat next to it.
Most did not in fact.
She could steal the beautiful right out of you;
Her soft flakes would melt on the tip of your
tongue,
And you were frozen,
In awe of her coldness.
Some found her chill appealing;
Her dangerous nature goes un-rendered,
And to many, her season is favored,
Desired by many.

Before Africa,
Snow added wonderful to whatever she landed
upon,
Making it somehow prettier than what it was
before.
The way she rested on a bare branch,
Like she was royal cloth wrapped around a
peasant.
It was a bony plain tree,
But when she aided to it,
It looked magical,
Enchanting it with her whimsical powers.
Her sparkle lit the tree,

So you would assume it better off.
Before Africa,
Nothing compared to snow,
Yet something changed.
I was in Africa struck in amazement at the beach.
It was late November in Durban, South Africa;
There was no hint of snow,
Just sand.
It was warm from the sun,
So I let my curious toes feel into it,
Searching through it,
Finding rocks and sea shells.
My feet bled into the sand,
Camouflaging themselves within it,
Along with the other bodies that surrounded me.
Sand clung to each one of them,
Not to outshine them but to be a part of them,
Molding herself onto us,
So we could all be beautiful together.
Snow never suited me;
It made my feet numb,
Its blinding white light made my eyes squint.
I always stood out.
My dark skin,
Next to such white.

Before Africa,
It was all I knew,
But once the sand warmed me,
I had forgotten all about winter.

Tales of a Poor Boy

Blisters rule over his tired dirt-ridden feet.
His path is never on course.
Instead he crisscrosses and zigzags his way to
a stranger.
Draped in rags that dangle effortlessly from
his skin,
And with every slight movement,
A piece of cloth finds another excuse to
remove itself from his body.
Uncovering his fragile flesh,
The bones ache to be free,
Poking at his skin,
Penetrating his body with force,
Angering forth to the surface.
His body now operates like that of a machine,
That is slowly running out of power,
But somehow keeps functioning out of shear
will to survive.
He knows only his small thirst for change.
His sister paces with the same routine except
she supports a newborn on her back,
And they roam together, through the endless
sea of sidewalks.
Hoping to greet a willing giver,
It is midnight and their weary eyes keep
searching, keep asking.
They wait in silence as their onlooker pears at
them in pity or disgust,

Debating if reaching in their pockets is worth their time,
Unaware that their choice is a matter of life and death.
Some give kindly, proud of the good deed for the day.
Others tell them to get a job or go to school—
Leaving them helpless, pleased with their generous advice.
But the child does not know such language,
Just yes or no.
Anything beyond this is hopeless to him.
Money is the key he has learned.
No parents to help him.
Maybe they left or maybe they died.
Looking in those eyes, I would be unable to tell.
Nothing resides in them.
The innocence and joy left him long ago.
Pain and suffering is all he knows,
Along with the hustle of the night.
This burden is far too great for such a poor boy.
I wanted to scream but relented,
I knew my scream would surely last forever.
Life as we all know it to be, is unfair,
Not discriminating on age, gender, or race,
It targets whomever it wishes.
So harsh even on this poor boy.
But I hope this child,

Will find a way of freedom,
Of this pain and suffering,
This night he does not belong in.
I settled within myself that I will see him
again.
In heaven I propose.
And there he will be,
His eyes filled with everything glorious,
And happiness is all that he knows.

Black Suit

In every closet
There is a black suit
Waiting to be worn
To stick to your skin
And makeover your mind
And so it has began
The wearing of power
The wanting of money
Until this black suit becomes
you
Forgetting who you were
before it
Hidden in the back of your
closet
The truth you used to wear
The clothes still dirty of
humanity
The stench of reality you refuse
to bear
Remains hung like lynched
flesh you crucified
Ashamed of the conscious that
once was
Of the conscious that should be
But the appearance of a black
suit consumes you
The manipulative tongue
The deceptive walk
The enticing talk
And the briefcase

Filled with unapologetic lies
And dollar signs
Your hair slicks back
And there is a chill in your eye
Because the coldness owns you now
Your shoe shines
But there is no reflection
Of a man anymore
You are something else
Resembling a bit of a monster
I can only watch you walk away
Into the nightmare you help dream

City Limits

There is a city within a city that none can speak of
Out of embarrassment or devious pleasure
I cannot say
But there are places that not even ghosts would dare go
In fear of such overwhelming scarcity
There is a quiet destruction
Unraveling more and more its disturbing truth
Abandoned buildings smile deadly
And the grass, some yellowed and old, rots in sorrow
While others, maddened and overgrown
Rise up in a hopeless rebellion
The glass, broken and shattered,
Remains lit from the sun
Giving off its best impression of diamonds
A devil's deception
To somehow make-believe something beautiful still remains
All that is crumbled and rusted

Has found contentment there
There is a devastating peace
Among the damned here
As we walk comfortably amongst it
Our heavenly hell

Troubled Black Woman

There is a troubled black woman
Suspicious of what the sun had done
When its yellow-stained rays
Painted her a darker shade
As if she but ash in life's grave
Obsessed in the obscurity
She set aflame amidst her own fury
Suddenly cursed
Isolated in her tragedy dispersed
Wallowing in her soiled complexion
Bleaching away at her flesh
A white obsession
Delighting in the ideology that lightness is simply
And utterly the epitome of beauty
Believing the fair-skinned holds the cure
While black skinned hollowed and impure
There is a troubled black woman
Seeping out an awful hatred from her pores
In a hurried sweat, the remnants of a war
A battle that has been long running
A battle unloving
To find some resolution to her black permanence

That she too is decorated in beautifulness
Hidden within herself
An identity unrealized
Waiting to explain
That there is nothing to be ashamed of
For there is no great evil resting within you
Nor some innate ugliness were you born to
Because like the night conflicted with the same black fight
Found solace in the shining of the stars
And the glowing of the moon
There is brightness within the darkness already
And all too many say
That the night is just as striking as the day
Find pride within that
To be dark but full of light
And oh the glory to such a promising sight

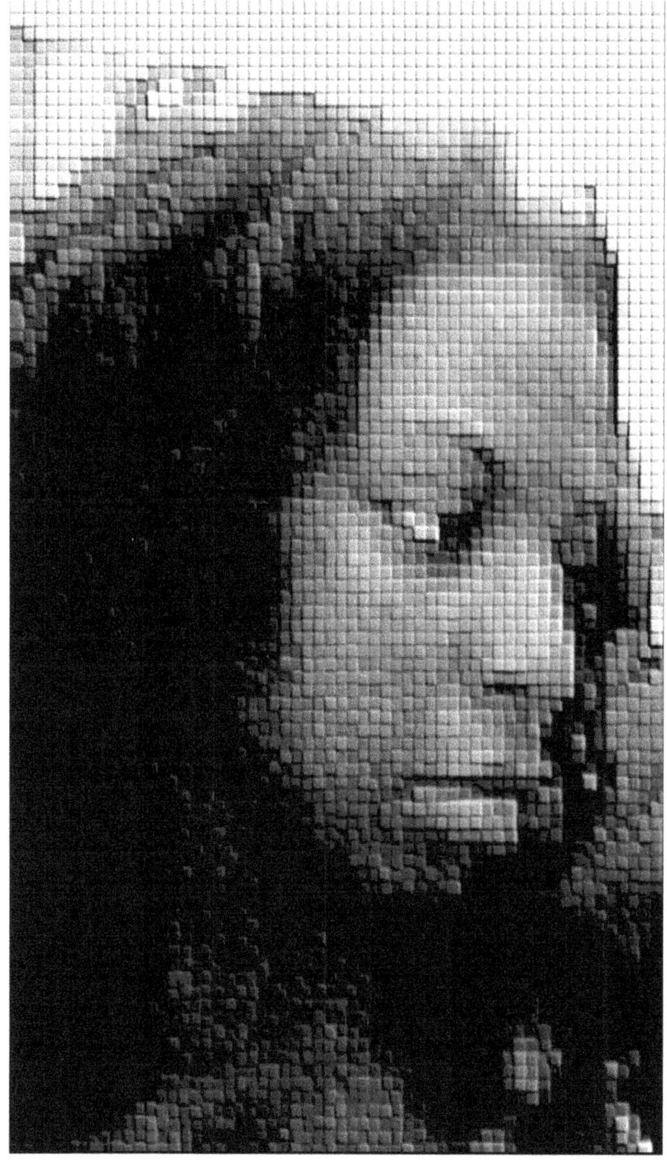

Forgiveness

I stand before **me**
To see myself walk into a troubled **destiny**
I close my eyes to awaken with a disturbing **epiphany**
Man holds my life in his **hands**
And in this **dance**
He suspends my life from a thread
Snatching the very essence of my soul
And entrapping it in a place unknown
Where it is lost, cannot be found
The shadow of death can no longer reach **me**
Because man has to teach **me**
That he is the true crypt **keeper**
I still begin to look **deeper**
Yes Father, I have come to you for I have **sinned**
To suffer my consequence, boldly man stands before Him to tell me that my life will **end**
But I remember you told me vengeance shall be **yours**
So why do I see man on the other side of the **door**
Return evil with **good**
Somewhere man **misunderstood**
To return **death** must have been the devil's last **breath**
Because to **kill** was surely not in our Father's **will**
Whenever a soul is lost, a soul could have been found
But then again, what is a soul to you
The dependence of vengeance is so profound in the minds of those
And the burden weighs so heavy
And I know their **hurting**
But we have to start **learning**
That God said vengeance is his, not yours
To **forgive** is to **live**
Not to be bound by **hate** and let it **dictate** my way
To **forgive** is to **live**
Not to be chained by **revenge**
Let thy God **avenge**
Gandhi once said an eye for an eye makes the whole world **blind**
Soon this world will no longer see
Then will never **find**

The path of a righteous **mind**
That billboard of peace on that highway **sign**
Or pull off on that road that left un-forgiveness **behind**
Because Gandhi also said forgiveness is an attribute of the **strong**
Because it is easy for the weak to retaliate for the temporary **wrong**
But only can a powerful **soul**
Forgive even when their heart is not fully **whole**
But what we all must see is that we all pay that freeway **toll**
Though we are required to pay a **price**
That struggle is the only way for a stronger **life**
For someone to take what you love is pain and **strife**
A sharp-edged **knife**
Cut deep into the flesh **twice**
Conquering death with **death**
Is like defeating cocaine then being hooked on **meth**
It's still the **same**
Nothing will **change**
Inside you say you're **satisfied**
But you know it's a **lie**
Because **inside**
Your heart still **cries**
Your soul still **hides**
So you put a body to **rest**
In hopes that you would no longer be filled with **mess**
But you wake up and realize
That the death didn't bring your son back
You realize that a wrongful murder
Won't bring your wife closer
You just get colder
As I get older, it gets **harder**
To witness the unnecessary **slaughter**
That's why I believe the death **penalty**
Is a man-made **destiny**
A destiny meant for **destruction**
When we act out of mere **frustration**
We must look to the virtue of patience

To let God be God

God is Love: A Love Letter For Anyone

God is love
This is my truth
God is love
It may not be your truth but it is the truth I live by
God is love
I say this because love does not dwell in everyone
If everyone had love, there would be no reason for God to exist
For if everyone had love, than hate would have no reason to exist
If love does not rule in you than its opposite does.
If you don't believe in religion, believe in the spiritual power of hate & love.
Slavery, Apartheid, and the Holocaust showed hate in its most blatant destructive form
Mandela, King, Gandhi showed love in spite of being surrounded by hates wrath.
How can love flourish when hate is so ever-present?
How can love thrive when hate sickens?
Everything but love dies
Everything that is love lives
Where love is...follow it
Because it will be a sad day when you lose it
Something spiritual lives in you that separates you from the ones who let hate rule
What drives us to hate
Hate for no apparent reason
To kill for no apparent reason
Bring destruction for no apparent reason
What drives us to hate

You can't explain such reasons unless you tap into a spiritual realm
I've tried to understand people who suppress and degrade a people
But their reasons are lost and even they can't find them
Who gave the right to decide someone else's freedom?
Yes.. money, power, and greed are reasons but merely branches connected to a root that derives from some inconvenient truth we choose to ignore
You say there is no God but you give yourself authority to act like one
What makes a man ready to kill for power and another man to uplift for power?
What makes a man lead a group of people to corruption and another man lead a group to freedom ?
What is in a man that becomes Hitler?
What is in a man that becomes King?
What drives us to hate?
There is a deeper realm that we refuse to acknowledge
If you can explain why people hate for no reason then tell me
What drives us to love
When there was no reason to love,
Show compassion to people we do not know,
To sacrifice ourselves for people we do not know ?
You cannot explain such reasons unless you tap into a spiritual realm
Some people risk their lives for a cause they could have ignored

What drives us to fight against corruption, injustice ?
Why do some people do it and others do not?
What drives us to love?
There is a deeper realm that you refuse to acknowledge
If you can explain why people love when they had no reason to then tell me

Love is to and for everyone
Love is equal
And if you are not in these things, you are not in love
If you are not in love than you are in its opposite
This is the cure I live by that surges through my veins when the world has been infected with hate and abandoned the law of love
Because love will win when everything else fails
Love will endure when everything else suffers
Love is what we live for

God is love
Because not everyone has it.
If everyone had love, there would be no reason for God to exist.
If everyone had love, then hate wouldn't exist
And if there are two sides...
whose side are you on?

Once Upon a Black Star

Born before the sun
And black before night
Was a chosen one
A victor of light
The black star won
And crowned the dark bright
Reigning for a time
A rarity at sight
Set aglow by the light
of the fluorescent moon
Flitting a dance
while grey clouds swoon
Hung against the midnight sky
Like a sparkling fly
Twirling to and fro
by and by
Like the breath and the sigh
Which made hearts cry
The black star was the soul
that brought heaven nigh
Existing within
a promising dream
Slowly to come undone
from the galaxy seams
A cut from the thread
of black stars hanged
To mute the song
the black star sang
The night
Who was envious
In the movement
The light
The dark bright
Of the black star

Burned with a jealously
And watched with a spiteful eye
To the death
The black star would surely die
Its rise to greed arose
Blossoming like a wilted rose
Looming over the luminance
The night
The betrayer
To kill the aspiring
The black star
The night's firstborn
No longer adorn
By the one
The Creator
Rumored throughout the earth
The suspicions of a death gave birth

The black star had it all
Which led to the fall
The brightness would disappear
And The darkness feared
With a longing eye
And a look as the last goodbye
To the moon, cloud, and the
infinite sky
But all too quickly it became a
distant memory
But believe me, the death of the
black star was a day of infamy

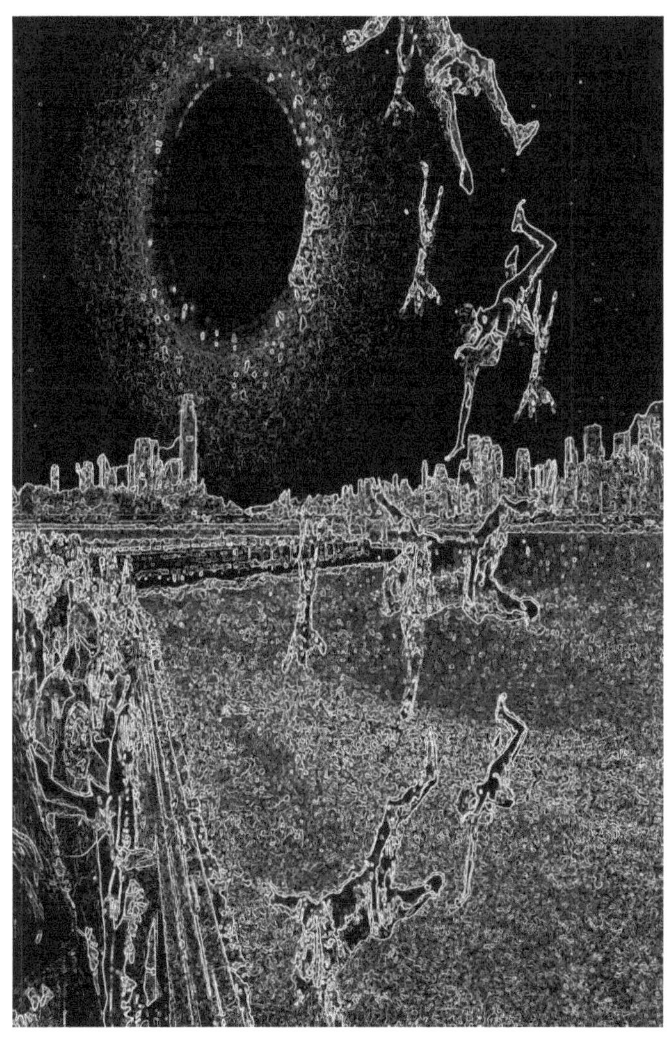

About the Author

Sharday Cage graduated from Saint Xavier University with a degree in Mass Communications. She currently resides in Chicago, IL, where she continues to pursue her passion as an up-and-coming writer and poet.

Sharday Cage began reciting her poetry at Saint Xavier, whereat she reached a pivotal moment: reciting her poem "Forgiveness" to Sister Helen Prejean, who has become a leading American advocate for the abolition of the death penalty and who was played by Susan Sarandon in the film based on her life, *Dead Man Walking*.

Sharday Cage has since taken part in plays around the Chicago area, such as *Tomorrow Never Came*, about the innocent lives lost to gun violence, and *As You Are*, an inspirational play. Sharday's poetry can be found at Record Magazine, an online poetry magazine which is dedicated to showcasing young poets, and at The Third City (thethirdcity.org).

Photo and Illustration Credits

Raudales-Richards, Gabriela

21, 43, 79, 89, 127, 135, 167

Wade, Matthew

67, 68, 151

You can find out more about Matthew Wade and his work at the following websites:

www.behance.net/matthewwade

http://www.imdb.com/name/nm3509137/

Additional photos, illustrations, and photo effects submitted by the editor, Sarah Engdahl

www.ingramcontent.com/pod-product-compliance
Lightning Source LLC
Chambersburg PA
CBHW060155070426
42447CB00033B/1476

* 9 7 8 0 9 8 4 6 7 8 5 2 5 *